INSTANT
Gardens

INSTANT
Gardens

PRACTICAL PROJECTS FOR
THE IMPATIENT GARDENER

PETER McHOY

LORENZ BOOKS

First published in 1999 by Lorenz Books

LORENZ BOOKS are available for bulk purchase, for sales promotion and for premium use. For details write or call the sales director: Lorenz Books, 27 West 20th Street, New York, NY 10011; (800) 354-9657.

ISBN 1 85967 888 2

Publisher: Joanna Lorenz
Project Editor: Joanne Rippin
Designer: William Mason
Production Controller: Joanna King
Reader: Hayley Kerr

Photographs by Peter McHoy, with additional material photographed by Peter Anderson, Jonathan Buckley, John Freeman, David Parmiter and Debbie Patterson. Photographs on the front cover and pp 66 & 67 top left and top right supplied by Harry Smith Horticultural Photographic Collection.

Printed in Hong Kong/China

1 3 5 7 9 10 8 6 4 2

CONTENTS

INTRODUCTION

Great gardens of the past were often designed and planted with the next generation in mind, especially where parkland was landscaped to blend in with the surrounding countryside, and avenues of trees or great yew hedges planted to reflect the grandeur of a large estate. In these days of small gardens and a more mobile population likely to move home several times, a more instant style of gardening is demanded. That doesn't mean less impact, just careful planning, appropriate plants, and projects that look good without having to wait years.

New gardeners, especially, are usually impatient for results, but even those of us with years of garden-making behind us still itch for instant results when moving house or simply redesigning an existing garden. Even if you plan some features that will take years to mature and look as you envisaged them, you still need lots of instant projects to transform your plot of land into something you're proud to call a garden.

There's nothing second-rate about an "instant" garden, and the projects and ideas that you'll find in this book will give you a garden to be proud of. It can be just as colourful and look just as lush as one that's taken decades to mature, and there are plenty of stunning non-plant projects that you can do in a weekend and that will give your garden a really well-designed look.

Opposite: *This trellis arbour can be made in a weekend. You can renovate an old seat or buy a new one, and most of the plants shown here are young shrubs or border plants with instant impact, or quick-to-flower annuals that may already be in bloom when you buy them. Transforming your garden can be as "instant" as that!*

HARD FEATURES FOR FAST RESULTS

You can buy summer bedding plants coming into flower that will provide colour and beauty almost instantly . . . if you happen to be planning and planting your garden in late spring or early summer. But you may be in your creative phase at some other season, and even if you start with an explosion of colour in summer, you'll need a framework of features to make your garden look interesting all year round.

It's a good idea to think first about the structure of your garden – its shape and form – then about hard landscaping features that you can add quite quickly. It's these that will probably transform your garden most dramatically, though, of course, you need a balance of plants too. There are plenty of projects in this book that you can follow or modify to suit your own garden or individual taste, and these will give your garden a finished look while the permanent plants are growing. Although "instant" plants are more difficult to find, unless you're prepared to pay for large specimens, there are lots of fast-growing plants that will clothe your garden in a season or two.

Creating hard landscaping, such as paving and raised beds, can be expensive and labour-intensive, but you don't have to tackle the whole garden in a season. Provided you work to an overall plan, different features can be built over a period of months or years, as time and budget allow.

Right: Drawing diagonals
This device creates a sense of space by taking the eye along and across the garden.

Far right: Formality with rectangles
A rectangular plan can be useful if you want to divide a long, narrow garden into smaller sections.

Left: *Include seating areas and sheltering arbours in your plan to make your garden welcoming.*

THINK ABOUT THEMES

Lots of gardeners think first about colour schemes for beds and borders, perhaps a blue and silver border, or a golden bed, but the best starting-point is the shape of beds, borders, paving and structural features such as ponds. This will give your garden a sense of unity and design.

You don't have to follow a rigid theme, and many splendid gardens just evolve, but if you need a few ideas, try working with circles, rectangles or diagonals. The permutations within each style are endless, but the designs illustrated here show how easy it is to create a striking garden using very simple shapes.

Left: Designing with circles
Circular shapes are effective in disguising or softening the predictable lines of the typically long, rectangular garden. Try various combinations in your designs, overlapping the circles if necessary.

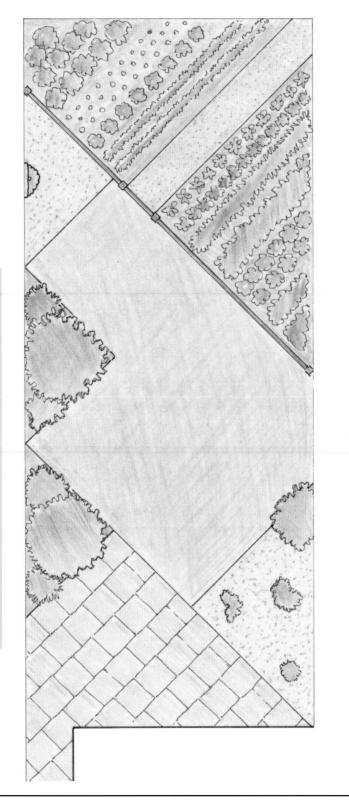

Be Bold with Boundaries

Don't allow your boundaries to let you down. Old wooden fences can look unattractive, and brightening these up, or replacing them with a hedge or a trellis, will transform a small garden.

QUICK HEDGES

The best-known fast growing hedge is **xCupressocyparis leylandii**, the leyland cypress, but it's too vigorous for most small gardens.

It's best to choose something more restrained if you want a fast-growing, low hedge for a small garden: try **Berberis thunbergii** varieties, shrubby honeysuckle (**Lonicera nitida**), or even common privet (the golden variety, **Ligustrum vulgare** 'Aureum', is more attractive and less vigorous).

PAINT THEM BRIGHT

Wood stains are available in a range of colours, and you may want to be bold and paint your closeboard fence green or blue, or whatever takes your fancy. A picket fence, like the one shown here, is often painted white, but you don't have to follow the herd. If you want to be adventurous, only your imagination will set the limit.

Right: *A smart coat of paint can improve a fence almost beyond recognition. Here sugar-almond shades differentiate the two properties, and the pastel pink matches the climbing roses.*

ERECTING A TRELLIS

1 Excavate a post hole at least 60 cm (2 ft) deep, using rubble to wedge the post upright while checking with a spirit level. Fill the hole with a concrete mix, ramming it in firmly, and checking periodically to ensure the post is still vertical.

2 Lay the panel on the ground, with one end close to the first post, to find the position for the next hole and post.

QUICK CLIMBERS

Although clematis and roses are understandably some of the most popular climbers, they are unlikely to provide good cover until at least the second year after planting. If you want a quick shrubby climber, consider the mile-a-minute plant or Russian vine (*Fallopia baldschuanica*, often sold as *Polygonum baldschuanicum*), honeysuckles, or the golden hop (*Humulus lupulus* 'Aureus').

For even quicker results, try growing one of the leafy annual climbers such as the variegated Japanese hop (*Humulus japonicus* 'Variegatus') or the canary creeper (*Tropaeolum peregrinum*), or in mild areas the cup-and-saucer vine (*Cobaea scandens*).

3 Nail the panel on to the first post, while someone else supports the other end. Use wedges of scrap wood or bricks to help support the panel temporarily. Check verticals and level.

4 Set the second post in position with concrete, making sure the tops of the posts align, and that the post itself is absolutely vertical. Nail the panel to it, then check levels and verticals again. Use temporary props until the concrete sets.

Above: *Make a feature of a trellis by bringing decorative panels out from the boundary into the border as a support for more climbing plants such as roses and clematis. Decorative panels like this make a strong visual feature, and will form part of an integrated design if linked with trellis boundary panels.*

Creating a Deck

Changing the garden floor can have a major and almost magical impact, especially if you do it creatively. And whether it's a new lawn that you're laying, paving that you're planning or designer decking, most of these jobs can be done in a weekend or two. The impact will be immediate, and will transform your garden much more quickly than waiting for plants to grow. Decking can be complicated to make, especially if you're making a raised deck in an elevated position, but here we tell you how to make a really simple deck from everyday materials such as fence posts and gravel boards (the boards placed at the foot of a wooden fence where it's in contact with the ground).

HOW TO MAKE A DECK

1 Level and consolidate the area to be decked, then use low-density building blocks or bricks to support your decking. Calculate the position of each row, bearing in mind that each timber bearer should be supported in the middle as well as the ends, if possible. Excavate so that about half the block sits in the soil – it's important that air circulates beneath the bearers.

2 Tap down each block to ensure it's level, removing more soil if necessary, or adding sand or sifted soil to raise an end that is too low.

3 Use a spirit level to ensure the blocks are level within the row and from row to row, otherwise the decking will be unstable. Place the level on a long straight edge to span between one row and the next.

4 You can use fencing posts for bearers, which should already have been impregnated with a preservative to reduce the risk of rot, but paint on a coating of wood preservative as an additional precaution.

Above: *Here the deck has filled most of a small town garden, but a border has been left around the edge for some green foliage. You could add colour with containers of flowers or just enjoy the simple, cool green effect.*

5 Space out the bearers to support the decking, adjusting them if necessary. It's worth providing extra support near the ends and sides of the decking, which is where the planks may need extra stability.

6 Your bearers may not be long enough to stretch the whole length of the deck, in which case make sure joints are made above a block or brick. Use a piece of damp-proofing strip between each block and bearer, to prevent water seeping up into the wood by capillary action.

Above: *A low, simple deck like this, perhaps for a patio area, will add lots of interest to your garden. You can stain it an attractive colour to make more impact – this deck has been stained a red cedar colour.*

7 To suppress weed growth, use a plastic sheet over any exposed ground, and give the timber an additional coat of preservative. Saw the decking planks to size and treat with a preservative. Nail in position with galvanized nails or use rustproof screws, leaving gaps of about 6mm (¼ in) between each plank to allow for expansion.

Designs on your Paving

An area of paving is not only practical, but gives a garden a more structured look instantly. And it need not look boring if you choose visually pleasing designs and finishes, and are prepared to mix materials for a more stylish result.

LAYING PAVING SLABS

1 Prepare a firm base by excavating to a depth that allows for hardcore (rubble), mortar, and paving. About 5–10 cm (2–4 in) of hardcore is adequate for foot traffic; you'll need 15 cm (6 in) for vehicles. Make sure both ground and hardcore are compacted.

2 Bed each slab on five blobs of mortar, using five parts sharp sand to one part cement. Or lay the slab on a solid bed of mortar, though this makes adjusting it more difficult.

3 Starting from a known straight edge, position each slab in turn. Tap the slab level, checking with a spirit level. Lay a small slope in one direction, to ensure rainwater flows away freely.

4 Unless the slabs are designed to be butt-joined, use scraps of wood to ensure an even space between each slab. A few days after the paving has been laid, point the gaps with mortar.

PLANTING IN PAVING

A large expanse of paving can look boring if it is not broken up visually. Try leaving out a few paving slabs in a position where you're unlikely to want to walk. Plant a shrub or a climber against a wall, then decorate the surface with beach pebbles. If you have an existing area of paving, it's often easy to lift a slab and break up the ground beneath to add a plant.

Where there's space, it's a good idea to let plants tumble over the edge of the paving, but don't allow them to become a hazard underfoot.

1 Lift one or two paving slabs, depending on their size. If they've been mortared into position, loosen with a cold chisel and club hammer, then lever up with the chisel or a crowbar.

2 If the slab has been bedded on concrete, break this up with a cold chisel and club hammer. Fork over the soil, adding garden compost or manure and a controlled-release fertilizer.

3 Plant your shrub, firming it in well, and watering thoroughly. Arrange beach pebbles or gravel to make the feature more attractive and reduce the chance of soil splashing on to the paving.

CHOOSING PAVING

For a patio, or any large paved area, paving slabs are often the first choice. They're quick to lay and come in a variety of shapes, sizes and finishes. Choose the surface finish of your slabs carefully, as this can make a significant difference to the appearance of your paving.

Some, like the ones used here, resemble real stone. For some situations, the smaller scale of bricks or clay pavers makes them a more suitable choice. In a cottage garden the colour and style of brick may be more in keeping with the age of the house than paving slabs.

Above: *Soften the effect of an area of hard landscaping such as paving by using plants that will spread over the edge a little, without causing an obstruction.*

Right: *You don't have to pave the whole area with the same material – a subtle mixture of paving materials can often make the garden look more interesting.*

In Place of Grass

It could be that the floor of your garden needs an uplift, so if you're tired of mowing grass but don't fancy more paving, why not consider the many merits of gravel?

A gravel area can be a straight substitute for grass (one that requires far less maintenance), or you could consider a gravel bed within part of a large existing lawn, making an interesting feature, perhaps following the theme of a Mediterranean garden, and still reducing the amount of mowing required.

If you are completely replacing an existing lawn, you can save having to dig it up by applying a weedkiller, installing an edging that rises slightly above the level of the old lawn, and simply covering it with gravel.

Below: *Sun-lovers like* dianthus and helianthemums, *which need good drainage, will thrive in gravel* .

HOW TO LAY A GRAVEL BED

1 Excavate the area to be covered with gravel to a depth of about 5 cm (2 in), but don't disturb the soil to a greater depth than you need to.

2 Lay heavy-duty black plastic (or a mulching sheet) over the area, to suppress weed growth. Overlap the strips by about 5 cm (2 in).

3 Barrow the gravel to the site and tip it over the base sheet. Rake it level.

4 You can plant through the gravel by drawing it away from the planting area and making a slit in the plastic or mulching sheet. It may be necessary to enrich the soil beneath with fertilizer if you've removed fertile topsoil during construction.

5 Firm the plant in, water well, then draw back the gravel around the crown of the plant.

CHOOSE YOUR COLOURS

Gravel comes in many shapes, sizes, and colours, so shop around until you find a type that suits your garden. Some are angular, others more rounded, some are white and very bright, others come in assorted shades of green or red and are more mellow. All will look different depending whether they are viewed wet or dry, in sun or shade.

Left: *Plant a gravel bed with Mediterranean plants for a drought-proof, fragrant garden. By forking plenty of gravel into the soil, as well as spreading it as a mulch, you will give them the free-draining conditions they need. Bulbs also love good drainage, and will provide dazzling accents of colour in your Mediterranean bed.*

Right: *Bear in mind the eventual spread of your plants when you plan the bed. The plants will quickly spread to fill the available space. Meanwhile, the gravel looks attractive in its own right, and helps to suppress weeds.*

Ways with Water

Few features will transform your garden as dramatically or as quickly as a water feature. Whether you buy a wall fountain kit that you simply screw to a wall, or make a pond for fish and waterlilies, within a weekend you can have the magic of the sight and sound of water. Site your pond carefully so that you can see it whether you are sitting indoors or out, and it will give you year-round enjoyment. If you have small children, opt for a feature that does not require any depth of water, such as a small fountain that drains through pebbles.

BIG IDEAS FOR SMALL FEATURES
Your water feature doesn't have to be large to create an impact.

If you use water with some imagination, it will become an instant focal point. Choose a size to suit your available space.

HOW TO MAKE A LINER POND

1 Mark the outline of your pond with a hose or rope, or by sprinkling a trail of dry sand from a bottle. Remove the grass and excavate the soil to the required depth, but leave a ledge about 23 cm (9 in) wide and deep around the edge for planting baskets.

2 If the pond is to have a paved edge, slice off a strip of grass around it, to the depth of the paving plus about 1 cm (½ in) for mortar. Use a spirit level on a straight edge to check the pond is level all round. It may be possible to span all around the pond from a central peg, otherwise you will have to set up a series of pegs around the edge.

3 Remove sharp stones and large roots, then line the excavation with about 1 cm (½ in) of damp sand (provided the sides slope slightly it should adhere). You may find it more convenient to buy a special polyester mat (usually available from the same sources as pond liners), which is laid before the liner itself.

4 Drape the liner over the hole, anchoring the edges with bricks. Run water into the pool from a hose. As the weight of the water takes the liner into the hole, release the bricks gradually. Some creases will form but are not usually noticeable later.

5 Trim the liner, leaving an overlap around the edge of about 15 cm (6 in) which will be covered by paving later.

6 Bed the paving on mortar, covering the edge of the liner. The paving should overlap the edge of the pool by about 3 cm (1¼ in). Finish off by pointing the joints with mortar.

Above: *If you have space for only a very small pool, try adding a miniature fountain, and perhaps an ornament for extra impact. Make sure the fountain is positioned so that the spray does not drift over the edge of the pool, even in windy weather.*

Above: *Amazing though it sounds, you can grow a waterlily in a large pot. It's best to choose a small variety or one that's not too vigorous, and of course the pot must be glazed. A wooden half-barrel can also be used this way.*

Right: *This formal pond works well because of its interesting shape and clever use of plants and ornaments. The pebble "beach" at one end provides easy access for wildlife.*

A Decorated Arbour

Arbours and pergolas provide a wonderful opportunity to extend your garden upwards by growing plenty of climbers, but they are also invaluable in design terms, dividing up your garden visually and suggesting different vistas and separate areas to explore. Well-positioned dividers can transform a garden's perspective while an arbour provides somewhere private to sit. Both offer a beautiful and fragrant part of the garden in which to linger if you plant scented climbers and shrubs around it.

MAKE AN ARBOUR

Transform your garden in a weekend with this charming arbour. Here's how:

1 You will need the following diagonal trellis panels: 3 panels 183 × 60 cm (6 × 2 ft), two for the sides and one for the top; 2 front panels 183 × 30 cm (6 × 1 ft); 1 front concave panel 183 × 46 cm (6 × 1½ ft); 1 back panel 183 × 91 cm (6 × 3ft). You also need 6 posts 7.5 × 7.5 cm (3 × 3 in), each 2.2 m (7 ft) long, and six metal post support spikes of appropriate size; 5 cm (2 in) galvanized nails and 3 cm (1¼ in) zinc-coated steel screws.

2 Start with the back panel, placing the posts 183 cm (6 ft) apart. Mark their positions, then drive in two spiked metal post supports with a mallet. Secure the posts into the metal "shoes" of the supports. Temporarily fix the top of the trellis by nailing to the top of the posts. Then drill and screw at intervals down each side of the trellis.

3 In the same way, position the front outside posts and fix the side panels, then the inside front posts and front panels. Screw the concave panel to the panels on either side of it, and finally screw the roof into the posts. Paint the arbour with an exterior wood stain.

Right: *An arbour makes a tranquil place to sit, or, if you draw up a table, an intimate setting for a meal in the garden.*

RUSTIC POLE CANOPY

Rustic poles are a popular choice for canopies, walks, pergolas and small arches, and assembling them is easy. Make almost any design using the joints shown here.

Right: *Rustic poles make an ideal support for climbing and rambling roses, though many other climbers are also suitable.*

1 Fix horizontal poles to vertical ones by sawing a notch of suitable size in the vertical pole to make a snug fit.

2 To join two horizontal pieces, saw opposing ends to match so that one sits over the other, then nail or screw them together.

3 Fix cross-pieces to horizontals or uprights by removing a V-shaped notch with a chisel. You may have to adjust the notch until it's a snug fit. Nail the poles into position.

4 Use halving joints where two pieces have to cross on the same plane. Make two saw cuts halfway through each pole, then chisel away the waste timber. Nail together.

5 A bird's-mouth joint is useful for connecting horizontal or diagonal pieces to uprights. Cut out a V-shaped notch about 3 cm (1¼ in) deep, then saw the other piece to match. If needed, chisel away more wood to fit.

6 Whenever possible, try the assembly on the ground first, then secure the uprights in prepared holes and concrete them into position. Nail or screw the upper pieces into position when the post concrete has set.

PLANTING FOR QUICK RESULTS

Compromise is no sin when it comes to planting your garden. Choose a mixture of plants: some for instant colour, others that may take a few months or even a year to look good, and a few "framework" shrubs and trees for the longer term. You'll have a garden to enjoy now and one that will look even better as each season passes.

It's easy to be tempted by summer bedding plants which are often already coming into brilliant bloom when you buy them, but packing your garden exclusively with these will leave some nasty gaps once autumn arrives. Even if you replant immediately with spring bulbs, there will be months of bare ground and boredom. Use these plants lavishly, but don't forget a few evergreens, quick-growing shrubs such as brooms (*cytisus*), and even fast-flowering rock plants such as *aubrieta*, to bridge the seasons and ensure a planting that looks balanced and is planned with year-round interest in mind.

In the following pages you will find lots of suggestions for ways to use different kinds of plants, but don't forget to mix and match wherever it seems appropriate. Use bulbs in the herbaceous or shrub border; use ground cover plants to suppress weeds in borders as well as in wilder parts of the garden. Seasonal plants are ideal for using in containers, but are less trouble to maintain in flower beds, and many can be used to fill in gaps in the herbaceous or shrub border.

Left: *Bulbs are great for the impatient gardener. Spring-flowering bulbs, especially, are almost certain to flower in their first season. Use them lavishly in beds and borders, but also pot up containers for maximum impact at the beginning of the season.*

Left: *For a gloriously rich, banked window display, one window box has been fixed to the front edge of the windowsill, while the other sits on the ledge. The planting scheme of petunias and dianthus bought from the garden centre a few weeks ago creates an instant impact when first planted, and a riot of colour later when the flowers bloom.*

Above: *Although container plants need regular attention and watering, you can move them around to enliven any part of the garden that's going through a dull patch. It will help if the containers themselves are decorative too.*

Right: *This scene has a suggestion of maturity about it, yet all the plants are young or can be bought as you see them here. The apple trained against the wall and the two pillar-like ballerina apples can be bought in flower like this, and, amazingly, you'll probably be able to enjoy a few fruits in the first season. The pot by the wall is planted with the moss-like* Soleirolia soleirolii: *a small plant can grow to this size within a month or two.*

Framework Trees

Plant a few shrubs, and even fast-growing small trees, to give your garden substance throughout the year. Many of these plants will be decorative in their first year, even though you will really be planting with the future in mind.

It's not difficult to plant shrubs: just make sure the ground is deeply dug with as much garden compost or rotted manure as possible, and plant with the top of the root-ball in a slight depression, to make sure water doesn't run to waste while the young plants are becoming established. Trees in borders can be planted in a similar way, but it's worth planting a small tree in a lawn to make a distinctive feature. Here, it will become a focal point, and even a small tree will have impact that might be lacking if planted elsewhere.

FAST BUT NOT RAMPANT
Although you want quick-growing trees, be sure to avoid those types that don't know when to stop. A classic example is the widely planted conifer **xCupressocyparis leylandii**, which is very fast-growing either as a tree or hedge, but often outgrows its welcome equally quickly. Choose trees with their ultimate height in mind, to make sure they will be right for your garden. Check the label or ask when you buy it.

HOW TO PLANT A LAWN TREE

1 Mark a circle 90–120 cm (3–4 ft) in diameter on the grass, using a trail of sand or a rope looped into a circle, then lift the grass with a spade, removing about 15 cm (6 in) of soil at the same time.

2 Insert a short stake before you plant, positioning it on what will be the side of the prevailing wind. Place it off-centre in the planting hole to allow the root-ball to occupy the central position.

3 If you buy a bare-root tree, instead of one growing in a pot, spread out the roots before trickling soil between them. Make sure the soil comes to the original soil-mark on the stem after planting. Use a cane laid across the planting hole to match the soil-mark to the final soil level, which should be about 5 cm (2 in) below the lawn.

4 Shake the stem occasionally as you return the soil, to settle it between the roots, then firm in well. Secure the tree to the stake, and water well. Consider mulching the bed to suppress weeds and to make it look more attractive.

Left: *It's best to prepare a special planting circle rather than attempt to have grass growing right up to the trunk of your tree. Shade will mean ordinary grasses won't grow well too close to the trunk, and mowing will be difficult under low branches.*

PLANTING IN A CONTAINER

Trees and shrubs do surprisingly well in a container, provided it's a large one. A half-barrel is ideal. Dwarf and slow-growing conifers are a good choice because most are ever-green, and the impact is apparent even while they are small. You can always plant them on in the garden later.

1 Choose a large container, such as a half-barrel, making sure it has drainage holes in the bottom. Cover these with broken pots and a layer of gravel. Add a layer of loam-based potting soil. This is better than a peat or peat-substitute type as you need weight for stability.

2 Place the plant, in its pot, in the middle of the container to check the planting depth. There should be a gap of about 2.5 cm (1 in) between the top of the soil and the rim of the container.

Above: *Choose the position for your container tree or shrub carefully, as these large containers are very heavy to move around once planted. If possible, fill the container after you have placed it in its final position. If you have to move it after planting use some rollers to make the job easier.*

3 Remove the plant from its pot, and gently tease out some of the roots from around the edge of the root-ball. This will encourage quick rooting into the surrounding potting soil.

4 Backfill with more potting soil, then water thoroughly. Top-dress with horticultural grit or fine gravel for a decorative finish and to reduce any evaporation from the surface.

BUYING BIG SPECIMENS

Most of the trees and shrubs sold in garden centres are young and relatively small specimens. These are the best choice if you're not in a hurry, and much cheaper too, but if you're prepared to pay the premium, consider looking for extra-large specimens.

There are specialists who can provide very large trees and shrubs, and many garden centres offer a limited range that are many years older than the plants they normally sell. These are likely to be very expensive and very heavy to move (you may need extra help with the planting), but you may consider it worth buying just one or two of these if you really want your garden to look more mature almost overnight. These trees will be too large to fit into your car, so you will need to have them delivered.

An Instant Lawn

Nothing has as much impact on the look of a garden as a really super lawn, and creating one can be as easy as laying a carpet.

If you've been thinking about a new lawn, go for turf rather than seed if you want instant results. A lawn from seed will take months to grow to a stage where it looks good and can be used, and it's much more of a chore to prepare and bring into a weed-free condition. Turf is more expensive, especially if you choose one grown from high quality grasses, but it's really instant, and should be weed-free from the start.

Another advantage of turf is that you can lay it at any time of the year, as long as the ground is not frozen, whereas seed is best sown in spring or autumn. Although your garden centre may stock turf, make sure it hasn't been allowed to deteriorate in storage. It's generally best to order from a specialist supplier, who will deliver it soon after cutting.

LAYING TURF

1 Dig and consolidate the ground, removing perennial weeds, at least a week before laying your turf. Leave it longer if possible, to allow the soil to settle. Before you begin, rake the soil surface level, then unroll the first strip of turf along a straight edge.

2 Stand on the turf, not the soil, as you lay successive rows, using a plank to distribute your weight. Stagger the joints between the turves to avoid creating the impression of an unbroken line.

3 Tamp down each row of turf as you progress (some gardeners use a special wooden tool for this, but the head of a rake works quite well).

4 Brush sieved soil (or a mixture of peat and sand) into the joints to help bind the turves together.

5 If you require a curved edge, lay the turf beyond the boundary initially, then cut back to the required shape using a half-moon edger (edging iron), with a hose or rope as a guide.

MAKING A MOWING EDGE

If your lawn is bounded by a border, make a mowing edge. It will mean the grass always has a neat edge, and you won't damage overhanging border plants when you mow. You can work this transformation with an established lawn as easily as a new one, using paving slabs or bricks. On a very large lawn, your edging can be wide, especially if you have large plants that are likely to flop over the edge. If the lawn is small, however, be sure to use a narrow edging so that it doesn't look out of proportion and dominate the grass.

1 Position the paving slabs on the grass and cut a straight edge with a half-moon edger (edging iron).

2 Slice away the grass with a spade, removing enough soil to allow for the depth of the slab or brick, about 2.5 cm (1 in) of sand and gravel mix, and about 1 cm (½ in) of mortar. Compact well with a hammer and piece of wood.

3 Use five blobs of mortar to bed each slab (it's best to lay bricks on a bed of mortar). Position the slab in place and tap level, using a mallet or the handle of a club hammer.

4 The slabs should be laid evenly, and flush with or very slightly below the lawn. Use a spirit level to check. Finish off by mortaring between the joints.

Left: *If you use quality turf and look after it, your lawn will rightly be a central feature of your garden.*

Multi-Coloured Carpets

Ground-cover plants will quickly clothe bare soil in a newly planted border, and help to suppress weeds too, so your garden will look mature surprisingly soon if you choose fast-growing plants such as bugle (*Ajuga reptans*). This is a good choice for a quick ground cover, as it naturally spreads in all directions and roots into the surrounding ground, forming a low-growing carpet of foliage which looks fresh all year round. There are many variegated varieties: the one shown here is 'Burgundy Glow'. *Ajuga* is a good choice because it covers the ground quickly, and will thrive even in unpromising places like damp soil and shade, but it's a spreader and may require thinning and replanting after a few years.

PLANTING GROUND-COVER

1 Space the plants while still in their pots initially, to make it easier to adjust the spacing if necessary. Staggered rows of plants will help your carpet to knit together quickly.

2 Close spacing will ensure quick cover, but if you have patience and want to economize, space the plants a little further apart. Knock each plant out of its pot just before you plant, using a trowel.

3 Firm each plant in well, making sure the surrounding soil is in good contact with all of the root-ball.

4 Water the plants thoroughly after planting, and make sure they remain moist until well established. *Ajugas* will spread rapidly, provided they are not allowed to dry out.

Left: Ajuga reptans *'Burgundy Glow', always a striking carpeter with its dark colours and strong variegation.*

Above: Ajuga reptans *'Catlin's Giant' is a distinctive variety with larger leaves and stronger growth.*

Below: Ajuga reptans *'Variegata', also known as 'argentea'.*

OTHER QUICK CARPETERS

If you don't fancy ajugas, try one of these other fast growing carpeters. Bear in mind that bcause some of these are fast-growers they may ultimately require some restraint. But even these plants are useful for quick cover while more permanent plants are becoming established.

Aegopodium podagraria 'Variegata'

This is a variegated form of the ground elder that many gardeners struggle with as a weed. It's actually an attractive plant with grey-green leaves edged with white. It's best used in a wild part of the garden, or where the roots are constrained by a path or wall.

Aubrieta deltoidea

Most gardeners know this spring-flowering plant with its flowers in shades of blue and purple, but not so many know of its potential as a ground cover. The plants are not expensive and widely available, and quickly cover the ground.

Cerastium tomentosum

Popularly known as snow-in-summer, because its white flowers almost smother the grey foliage. Again it's inexpensive, and covers the ground quickly, but may become straggly.

Euonymus fortunei

This widely available shrubby plant (there are many variegated varieties) is usually planted as an isolated shrub, but they also make an excellent ground cover. They're not that fast-growing, but by planting close together you can create an instant, evergreen effect.

Lamium maculatum

Also known as the dead nettle, this very fast carpeter will grow almost anywhere, and spreads rapidly. There are several variegated varieties, some with mainly silver leaves that are good in shady areas. Self-sown seedlings can be a problem in future years.

Below: Cerastium tomentosum.

Break up a Lawn

If you think your garden looks plain, and it has a large area of grass, you may decide that the lawn needs a feature to break the garden up visually. An island bed is a good choice for instant impact, and also offers the added benefit of an opportunity to grow more plants.

MAKING AN OVAL BED

To make an accurate oval, first mark out a rectangle to the overall dimensions. Place a peg halfway along each side and stretch string between them across the centre of the rectangle.

Cut a piece of string half the length of the rectangle and, using a side peg as a pivot, insert pegs where it intersects the string down the centre.

Measure the distance between one of these inner pegs and the further end of the rectangle. Make a loop from a piece of string twice this length. Drape the loop around both inner pegs and insert a bottle filled with dry sand. Holding it taut, walk round the pegs to mark the oval outline.

MAKING A FREE-HAND OR CIRCULAR BED

1 Provided the bed does not have to be exactly symmetrical, and you can trust your eye for an even curve, just lay a hose or rope to mark the shape of the bed. If you are using a hose in cold weather, run warm water through it first to make it supple – a cold hose is difficult to lay without making kinks.

2 Once you are satisfied with the profile, run sand along the marker (try filling a bottle with dry sand), then use a half-moon edger (edging iron) to cut the new edge. Lift the surplus grass, then dig over the soil, incorporating garden compost or rotted manure to improve the soil structure and fertility. Rake in a balanced fertilizer.

If you simply want to make a circular bed, a quick and easy method is to insert a peg in the centre and attach a string with loops at each end. Attach one end over the peg, and insert a bottle filled with dry sand at the other end, from which you can trickle out the sand.

Left: *This lawn looks all the more interesting for the small beds cut into it. Here, one has been planted with a shrub, the other filled with gravel as a standing ground for a collection of pots.*

Below: *If your garden is in the informal style rather than based on formal rectangles, the grass will probably look much more interesting with beds cut into it. This is something you can do to transform an existing lawn that looks a little boring. Plant with shrubs for long-term interest, or use seasonal bedding for instant impact, as in the small circular bed in the foreground.*

Above: *Sometimes it can be more effective to cut out a bed towards one end of the lawn, rather than in a central position. This can make the most of your lawn by taking the eye across it to the flower bed.*

Lovely Lilies

Lilies make lovely border plants, and you can buy them in pots already coming into flower in most garden centres throughout the summer. These are ideal for your "instant" border, and they'll come up again each year, so you are also making a very worthwhile investment.

Because lilies are such a long-term investment, making bigger and bolder clumps each year, it's worth giving them some special care and attention and working some garden compost or rotted manure into the soil before planting. It's also probably worth using a general flower fertilizer.

Dead-head the lilies after flowering, and, if the weather is dry, water the plants even after flowering is over, to make sure they become established for a repeat performance next year.

1 Make sure the potting soil is moist and space the plants while still in their pots, so that you can adjust the spacing easily if necessary. Plant close together for instant impact, further apart if you're looking ahead to large clumps as the bulbs multiply in future years. An odd number of plants usually looks best.

2 Knock each plant out of the pot by holding the potting soil with your fingers while inverting the pot. If the root-ball doesn't come out easily, give the edge of the pot a sharp tap on a hard surface.

3 Plant with a trowel, keeping the root-ball intact. There are often several bulbs in each pot – don't try to separate them out. Plant the root balls so that you have to cover the top with about 2.5cm (1 in) of soil.

4 Firm the soil around the root-ball, making sure there are no large air pockets that could allow the roots to dry out.

5 Water each plant thoroughly, making sure the root-ball absorbs moisture as well as the surrounding soil.

Above: *Lilium 'Chianti'*

Opposite: *Pot lilies are usually sold with the flowers in bud. Within days, you could have a display like this in your border.*

Spring Bulbs

It's hard to imagine spring without bulbs. The first snowdrop, early aconites, drifts of daffodils and showy tulips all help to dispel winter chill and fill us with the promise of better times.

INDOOR BULBS

If you are planting "prepared" bulbs for early flowering indoors, get them in early. Plant unprepared bulbs in containers at the same time to bloom later, giving you a succession of flowers. An odd number of bulbs in each pot looks best.

1 Part-fill your pot or bowl. If the container has no drainage holes, use a special bulb mixture.

2 Place an odd number of bulbs, such as three or five, on the potting soil. These are hyacinths.

3 Add more potting soil or bulb mixture around the bulbs, leaving their "noses" just exposed. Water, but be careful not to over-water.

4 Keep the bulbs in a dark, cool place until the shoots emerge. You could place them in a shady position outdoors, and cover them with sand. Remember to check them periodically.

PLANTING OUTDOORS

Spring-flowering bulbs may take six months from planting to flowering, but this is not long in gardening terms, and for most of that time you won't be out in the garden much anyway. Just plant them and forget them – until suddenly those shoots emerge, full of the promise of spring. You can even cheat and buy "prepared" bulbs for planting indoors. These will flower within three months, sometimes sooner, bringing spring into your home even while it's still winter outside. Bulbs treated for early flowering include daffodils and hyacinths.

1 Before planting in the autumn, dig or fork over the ground, removing any weeds. Incorporate plenty of organic material, such as garden compost or well-rotted manure, and add a very slow acting fertilizer such as bonemeal.

2 Unless you are interplanting bulbs with spring bedding plants such as wallflowers or forget-me-nots, it's best to make a hole large enough to take a group. For most bulbs it should be about three times the depth of the bulb (or corm or tuber).

3 Space the bulbs evenly. Close spacing will make a bolder show, but you'll need to buy more bulbs. Using the rake, draw back the soil over the bulbs, taking care not to dislodge them.

4 Mark the area with sticks or canes if you are likely to cultivate the area. Then insert a label.

Right: *You can almost always find space for spring bulbs in your borders. They'll provide interest before the herbaceous border plants take over.*

Above: *Hippeastrums (amaryllis) are among the most spectacular of all indoor bulbs, and they grow at an amazing rate.*

Summer and Autumn Bulbs

Most gardeners plant at least a few bulbs to flower in spring, but those that flower in summer and autumn are often neglected. This means you miss some wonderful plants that are easy to grow and often flower relatively soon after planting. Most modern hybrid lilies will flower in their first summer.

For autumn flowering, the impatient gardener must put colchicums top of the list. They're often coming into flower even before they're planted. Plant in late summer or early autumn, and they will probably be in flower within weeks. Grow them in partial shade at the front of a shrub border, or naturalize them in grass.

NATURALIZING COLCHICUMS

1 You can plant your colchicums (often called autumn crocuses) in the usual way in a border, but you can also naturalize them in grass. Plant them in a natural-looking drift.

2 Use a special bulb-planter or a trowel to make the holes. These should be at least twice the depth of the corms.

3 Insert the corm, then return the soil and top with the plug of grass removed. If a plug has been removed with a bulb planter, it will probably be necessary to remove some of the soil from the bottom before replacing it.

Left: *Colchicums do well beneath not-too-shady deciduous trees and shrubs. The flowers appear before the leaves, which follow in spring.*

Opposite: *Whether planting in grass or in a bed or border, try to plant colchicums in a bold drift. The corms will multiply over the years to give an ever-better display.*

Quick Cover-ups

If you're impatient to cover a bare or ugly wall, whether it's the side of your house, garden shed or the garden wall, grow a quick climber or shrub over an attractive trellis. The trellis will improve the appearance of the wall instantly, even while the plant is still small, and if you choose suitable fast-growing plants there will soon be good foliage cover. If it would suit the wall you are covering, you could consider painting the trellis a bright colour.

FIXING A TRELLIS

1 Once you've decided on the best position for your climber, drill holes at suitable intervals to take supporting wooden battens. Insert wall plugs to take the screws.

2 Use rustproof screws to secure wooden battens to the wall. The battens will hold the trellis away from the wall, allowing space for the stems to grow behind, and improving air circulation around the plant.

3 Nail the trellis firmly to the battens. If it's a wooden trellis, try to keep the base out of direct contact with the soil to reduce the risk of rotting.

4 Fork over the area in front of the trellis, incorporating plenty of organic material such as garden compost or (as here) spent mushroom compost.

5 Dig the planting hole at least 45 cm (18 in) away from the wall: closer in, the soil will stay very dry. Fork in a handful of bonemeal.

Right: *The golden hop is a prolific climber that will smother a large wall or fence with fresh-looking golden foliage. The old stems will need to be cut down to ground level each winter. They will die back naturally, and only require tidying up once they've collapsed and begun to look bedraggled.*

Above: *Climbers with twining stems, like this hop, wind themselves round any support, so once you've given them their trellis they'll look after themselves. Annuals, and those perennials that die back each year, such as the golden hop, will have to be disentangled to leave the trellis clear for new growth the following season. You'll find it easier to pull the old stems clear if you wait until the growth dies back of its own accord first, and by that time the leaves will have dropped off so you can see what you're doing.*

Left: *Honeysuckles are fast growers but still take a year or two to settle down. Large-flowered clematis usually produce a few blooms in their first year, but aren't so good at covering up. Try planting the two together for a happy combination. Most large-flowered clematis require annual pruning, so bear this in mind when choosing varieties. Those that flower in late summer on growth produced in the current year are the easiest to deal with than growth between other plants. These are simply cut back to about 23–30 cm (9–12 in) above the ground in late winter. You can then pull the old clematis stems free of the honeysuckle before it starts into new growth.*

Annual Climbers

Make the most of annual climbers, especially if you need quick vertical cover while you're waiting for your perennial plants to become established. You can use annuals to grow up wigwams or other supports in the border, or grow them up a light trellis to enliven a plain wall.

PLASTIC NET SUPPORTS
Most annual climbers will happily grow up a large-mesh net, but they can be difficult to disentangle from flimsy netting at the end of the season. If you're likely to grow climbers against the same wall next year, a more rigid type of plastic netting is best. These supports are available in several colours: choose the one that will blend most discreetly with the colour of your wall.

Left: *The canary creeper (Tropaeolum peregrinum) has pretty yellow flowers, but it's also a leafy annual with good screening qualities.*

1 Spacers should be used to hold the net away from the wall, and these are usually sold by the supplier of the netting. Some come with a masonry nail that you drive into the wall. Otherwise drill a hole, plug it, and fix the spacer or clip into the hole.

2 Use a spirit level to make sure the spacers or clips are aligned accurately, otherwise the net may not sit squarely against the wall.

3 Smooth the net down and mark the positions of further clips or spacers, at intervals of about 60 cm (2 ft) down the wall. You may need to move the net out of the way temporarily while you fix the clips to the wall.

Above: *If the perennial golden hop is not fast-growing enough for you, consider the annual Japanese hop (*Humulus japonicus*). This is a variegated form, showing how much cover it can provide within a couple of months.*

Above: *Use sweet peas to add height to a herbaceous or mixed border. You can use wire netting looped around tall canes for support, but twiggy pea sticks make a pleasing support for a season.*

Above: *The cup-and-saucer vine (*Cobaea scandens*) needs to be started off in the greenhouse and won't survive the winter outdoors, but it makes a mass of growth in a season, and the flowers are a beautiful bonus.*

Gap Fillers

Perennial border plants and shrubs usually take several seasons to look really good, while most annuals and summer bedding plants are in flower almost as soon as you've planted them out, but last only one season. Compromise by planting fast-growing seasonal plants between your perennials. You won't sacrifice colour or impact while the long-term plants are growing – and you won't have to replant every year.

Try to strike a balance between low-growing plants that bloom very quickly, such as French marigolds and pot marigolds (calendulas), and taller, bushier plants that flower later, such as cosmos and dahlias (dahlias are perennials, but some types can be raised from seed and are usually discarded after flowering).

PLANTING IN THE BORDER

1 Don't plant if the potting compost in the trays is dry. Water thoroughly first, allow plenty of time for it to soak in, then remove the plants from the tray.

2 Position summer bedding plants on the soil surface initially, so that adjustments are easy to make if necessary. Allow for the growth of the permanent occupants of the border.

3 Plant with a trowel, burying the root-ball slightly deeper than it was in the seed tray. Pull some soil back over the top of the root-ball to reduce the risk of the potting soil drying out. Firm in well.

4 Water well after planting, and in dry spells for the first couple of weeks. Where practical, be prepared to dead-head flowers as they fade, to extend the flowering season.

GOOD ANNUAL GAP FILLERS
African marigolds
Californian poppies (eschscholzia)
Cleome (spider flower)
Coreopsis 'Early Sunrise'
Cosmos bipinnatus
Dahlias (particularly bedding types)
Gypsophila elegans
Lavatera (annual mallow)
Pot marigolds (calendulas)
Rudbeckia (annual type)

Opposite: *Many bushy annuals are ideal for filling out a new border while young perennials become established. Here* Petunia *'Prime Time' is mingling with a perennial agryranthemum.*

Pots of Colour

Use containers lavishly for an instant injection of colour. You can pack them with seasonal bedding plants and spring bulbs, and if necessary move them around the garden to brighten up the inevitable dull spots you'll have while waiting for the more permanent plants to grow and mature to flowering size.

Left: *Spring-flowering bulbs should be used extensively if you want relatively quick colour. Although it will be several months before they flower, you'll probably spend little time in the garden during these winter months. Bunch-flowered narcissi make a cheerfully full-looking container.*

Below: *It's a good idea to plant winter-flowering pansies with dwarf spring bulbs such as crocuses. These flower whenever the weather's mild enough, and prevent the containers looking bare in winter.*

Left: *Over the years, auriculas have been hybridized to produce a stunning variety of flower colours, as well as subtle shades of brown, green and even black. Their velvety petals and intriguing markings merit close inspection, so grow them in pots where they will catch the eye. Inventively decorated containers are a match for the paintbox-bright colours of these flowers.*

Below: *Fuchsias will be a sure-fire success for summer colour, and from late spring onwards you buy them in flower. For a feature plant, invest in a standard, which will make more of a focal point. Choose an attractive container, and improve the feature still more by planting trailers around the base.*

Right: *It can take several years for shrubs and border perennials to make large specimens, and for your garden to look mature. You can speed things up by using ornate containers that also add height and look old, along with a few small shrubs in pots to fill in any obvious gaps. The stones make the group appear filled out.*

Above: *Groups of large containers can become a significant part of the garden's structure. Here they define the shape of the paved area as well as adding accents of seasonal colour. At the end of flowering, containers can be moved to a less prominent part of the garden while other pots take their place for the next season.*

Pond Plants

Although you can make a pond in a weekend, it takes longer to create a well-planted look. Waterlilies may take at least a couple of years to flower well, and many other choice aquatic plants are slow. Plant some of these for future displays, but choose some of the fast-growers to pack in the interest in the short term.

Many fast-growing pond plants can be used to soften and mask the edge of the pond, and to help it merge with the surrounding landscape. The downside to such vigour is that you may have to trim them periodically.

PLANTING MARGINALS

Marginal plants live around the edges of the pond, usually with their feet in shallow water, though some will also grow in moist soil outside the pond. They are usually planted with 2.5 cm (1 in) of water over the crown. Most marginal plants are planted in aquatic planting baskets, which should be filled with a heavy loam that's not rich in fertilizers or organic matter (you can buy aquatic soil if necessary).

PLANTING BOG PLANTS

If you can create a moist area around the edge of your pond, you'll be able to grow bog plants or those that thrive in moist soil, to give the pond a natural look. The plant shown here is *Houttuynia cordata* 'Chameleon', which is so adaptable that it will grow in an ordinary border, a bog garden, or in the water. Most bog plants are less adaptable.

1 Excavate a hole large enough to accommodate the root-ball of your plant. If the ground is dry, try to work in plenty of moisture-retaining humus-forming material such as rotted manure, garden compost, or peat.

2 Water the plant in its container and allow to drain, then knock it out of its pot. Place it in the planting hole, which may have to be adjusted for depth.

1 Line a pond basket with a piece of hessian or horticultural fleece, unless the holes in the side are very small. Part-fill the container with soil, then position the plants and trickle more soil carefully around the roots.

2 Cover the surface with gravel to help protect the soil from erosion and disturbance by fish. Lower the basket into the water gently, so that it sits on a marginal shelf that should have been built into your pond.

3 Firm the plant in, then water well. Be sure to keep well watered for the first few weeks, especially if dry weather follows.

Right: *The striking* Carex elata *'Aurea' (Bowles' golden sedge) grows relatively quickly, and even a small clump of it beside a pond will have a big impact.*

FLOATERS

For the group of plants known as floaters, planting couldn't be easier. You just place them on the surface of the water and let them float (like the water hyacinth, **Eichhornia crassipes**, shown here).

The water hyacinth is one of several fast-multiplying tender floaters (water lettuce, **Pistia stratiotes**, is another good one), which will cover a large area of water by the end of the season. But as they'll be killed off when the cold weather comes, they won't become a nuisance.

The same can't be said of duckweed (*Lemna* species) which is hardy and soon becomes a problem with its rapid spread.

FINISHING TOUCHES

No matter how vital plants are to a garden, it's often the outdoor furniture and ornaments that give it sparkle and a sense of individual creativity, stamping the garden with your personal style. The great merit of creative garden decoration for the impatient gardener is that the results are instant. A boring corner can be brought to life with a suitable ornament, a pretty patch can be enhanced even further with an attractive seat, quite ordinary plants can be made to look good in an interesting or unusual container, and by adding a few garden lights you can extend the hours of pleasure that you'll get from your garden, whatever the season.

Such improvements need not be expensive. Existing objects can be recycled, a pot of paint can often work wonders, and you may be able to make some of the projects described in the following pages from scrap material that you already have in the house or potting shed.

Left: You can turn what might be dismissed as old junk into an instant focal point. An old barrow and discarded galvanized metal watering can will suddenly create a corner of nostalgia when placed in juxtaposition. Add some old clay pots and just a few simple plants such as pansies, and suddenly you have a striking and adaptable garden feature.

Left: Magical moments can be created for a twilight party in the garden by something as simple and temporary as Victorian night lights, suspended from a tree with wire.

Right: A plastic chimney pot makes a practical planter, but it will look better disguised as an old lead chimney. This one was created with a coat of white acrylic primer followed by charcoal-grey emulsion, then painted randomly with acrylic scumble glaze tinted with white emulsion. It was finished off with a polyurethane varnish.

Above: *Get more out of your garden by using it after dusk. You can install electric lighting or simply depend on candle power for a romantic mood.*

Right: *A well-planted terracotta urn will make a striking focal point in your garden.*

Colour and Flair

It's not only plants that provide colour in the garden – you can do your bit with a paintbrush. Be prepared to be bold if you want real impact.

Some of these suggestions, such as painting your walls in bright colours, may take a little courage, but the results can be stunning, and it's one way to give your garden impact that plants would find it hard to match even when mature. Start with painting some pots and see what a difference that can make.

Left: *These small lily-of-the-valley plants would have looked pretty in a plain terracotta pot. But painting the clay pots white and covering the surface of the soil with moss has made them a really elegant garden feature for the spring.*

Above: *If your entrance lacks impact, get out the paintbrush. Painting a wall white will reflect light into a dull area, and it makes a flattering backdrop for plants. To introduce some colour around the door, this wall has been painted with brightly coloured stripes and pattern. Use a stencil for the leaves.*

MEXICAN PAINTED POTS

To bring vibrant colour to a hot, sunny patio you need something really bold. A series of stylized folk motifs painted over stripes of sizzling colours will give your terracotta pots a Mexican look when filled with flowers in dazzling colours.

1 Use strips of masking tape to cover the stripes that you have decided will remain terracotta, varying the widths. Then paint the main body of the pot with a white undercoat.

2 Once the undercoat has dried, paint the different coloured bands using gouache poster paints.

3 Peel off the masking tape when the paint has dried, exposing the bands of terracotta beneath.

4 Use a fine artist's brush to paint simple motifs, using white undercoat. When completely dry, coat with polyurethane varnish.

Above: *Pots like this will compete for attention with the brightest flowers in your garden, and are satisfying to create.*

Unconventional Containers

If a container is interesting enough, even young plants will pack plenty of punch, and you'll have an eye-catching feature from the day you plant it up.

If you look around your home and garden, you are almost sure to find everyday objects that can be turned into unusual and interesting containers for plants. Here are two possibilities to get you thinking.

VERDIGRIS BUCKET

There's no need to throw away old galvanized buckets when you can turn them into plant containers like this, but be sure to make drainage holes in the bottom first. To make the rust bucket shown behind the verdigris one, substitute rust-coloured acrylic paint for the aqua-green.

1 Sand an old galvanized bucket, then prime with a metal primer. Wait for two to three hours for this to dry, then paint with gold paint and let that dry for two or three hours.

2 Next, paint with amber shellac and allow it to dry for half an hour. Mix aqua-green and white acrylic paints to produce a verdigris colour, and add water to make a thin consistency. Sponge on the verdigris paint and let it dry for an hour or two. Finally, apply a coat of polyurethane varnish.

TIN-CAN TOWER

1 Paint a board about 60 × 30 cm (24 × 12 in) with undercoat and one or two coats of gloss paint, leaving the paint to dry between coats.

2 Clean some empty tin cans and remove the paper labels. Using metal cutters, cut down one side, and cut round half of the base so that you can open out part of the can.

3 Use pliers to open out the sides, then cut a V-shape into each side using metal cutters. Fold in the back half of the can base, and pierce the other half using a nail and hammer.

4 Arrange the cans on the painted board and secure by hammering a tack through each metal flap.

Above: *Ordinary cans look good on this wall feature, but if you can find some with pretty printed designs it will be even more colourful.*

In Suspense

Most gardeners use hanging baskets or wall pots to decorate their gardens, but most of the thought and effort usually goes into the planting, which can take many weeks to make a worthwhile display. If you choose an interesting or unusual container, you'll have something good to look at from the moment you hang it up.

Above: *The most unlikely items can be used as hanging baskets. This metal lantern from the Middle East simply holds a handful of ivies in terracotta pots to make a surprising and effective decoration.*

Left: *This hanging container with a difference looks all the better for being suspended from an old angled post. The plants are growing in an old copper builder's bucket from France, and its rich verdigris patina blends beautifully with the blue-green leaves of the oxalis and dianthus. Although subtle, the bright dianthus flowers draw the eye to this fascinating feature.*

GRECIAN HEAD

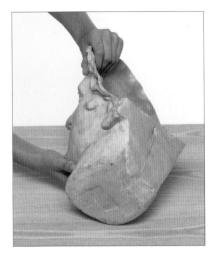

1 Make sure your wall pot has a hanging hook or hole, and provide a strong support on to which you can hook it.

2 Place a layer of expanded clay granules in the base to support the pot at the right level.

Above: *Although the petunia in this basket is still relatively small, this hanging feature makes a strong focal point because of the unusual container. Hanging a lantern from the same bracket means that the planting can be softly illuminated in the evening.*

3 Position the pot inside the wall pot, angling it slightly if necessary, to ensure the plant presents itself well to the front when the head is in position. Arrange the foliage to make a convincing leafy crown of hair, trimming off any shoots that are too long.

Right: *An Indian birdcage is an unusual candidate for a garden decoration, but it's full of character and interest, and a single potted plant is all it needs to catch the eye.*

Making Patterns

Striking patterns will give your garden a strong sense of design that will keep it looking interesting even during the winter months. Details like this make a garden special. An attractive edging to an otherwise ordinary path, a small but interesting feature such as a decorative tile, a pretty mosaic set into a path or wall, anything that arrests the eye, will make your garden interesting and individual. The features suggested here show how to use strong patterns to make your garden interesting.

This kind of project brings immediate improvements while you're waiting for the surrounding plants to grow. Train yourself to look for interesting materials to create original designs, and to think of ways to use objects that already have strong patterns.

AN ALPINE WHEEL

Although the wheel shown here is planted with alpines, you could fill it with herbs instead.

The symmetry of the feature is more important than what you plant in it.

1 Mark out the circle using a length of string the radius of your bed with a peg tied at each end. Then dig the area, incorporating plenty of garden compost and a dressing of a balanced fertilizer.

If you can find an old circular drain cover, use this as the centre of the wheel, and lay rows of bricks for the spokes. Place a rim of bricks around the circle, pushing out a little further into the surrounding area if necessary to avoid cutting bricks for the spokes.

2 Position your plants on the surface first, bearing in mind their likely spread after a year. If necessary, adjust the spacing before planting.

3 Cover the surface of the soil with fine gravel, and place some decorative stones between the plants as a finishing touch.

Below: *See how effectively an ordinary path can be transformed into a fantastic feature with a little imagination. You may have scallop shells like these left over from the dinner table, or you could perhaps make friends with your fishmonger.*

Above: *It's amazing how a few tessellated tiles, rescued from a crumbling city pathway and destined for a builder's skip, can have so much impact when set into a flower bed.*

4 The wheel will make a strong focal point, and will look good from the day it's planted. This one is about 2.4 m (8 ft) wide: adjust the size to fit your own garden.

Sitting Pretty

If you don't have time to sit in your garden you won't have time to appreciate it. So make time to enjoy the fruits of your labours – but first work a few speedy transformations on some seats that have seen better days.

By painting or putting fresh covers on old chairs, you can keep costs down and produce some really stunning and individual pieces of garden furniture at the same time. You may be able to rejuvenate old kitchen chairs, or perhaps pick up bargains from junk shops.

Above left: *The style of this chair is reminiscent of a traditional Tyrolean design, and its lavish decoration is perfectly in keeping with the strong colours of the summer garden.*

Above right: *This subtle colouring looks wonderful with glaucous and purple foliage, and teams up with the painted wall of the shed behind.*

Right: *Don't discard old deck-chairs that simply need recovering. You can buy striped deckchair canvases ready to nail on, but you can also create your own designs on plain canvas. Use stencils or draw a freehand design, using stencil paints or soft fabric pens.*

Above: *This traditional slatted chair has been painted in a soft, muted shade, at one with the silvery tones of its surroundings.*

Left: *Re-covered old chairs in bright colours look lovely in the garden but won't stand up to inclement weather.*

Above: *Some might have thrown out this old Lloyd loom chair, but instead it's been transformed into an interesting garden feature using two shades of blue spray-on car paint. Although the chair is very worn, it looks comfortable and makes an appropriate decoration for a cottage garden.*

Garden Ornaments

Use ornaments and features such as arches to transform dull or uninteresting parts of the garden into instant focal points. You don't have to wait for plants to grow, the effect is immediate – and they'll provide year-round interest in the way that few plants can.

Left: *An understated ornament like this little animal running along the top of a wall might not make a huge impact, but in a small garden, with the right background, will make a charming addition.*

Above: *This kind of feature is ideal for a shady corner where the emphasis usually has to be on foliage plants. A pedestal fountain brings the sight and sound of water to emphasize the sense of cool lushness, and adds the kind of height a design like this needs. You'll also find the water will attract birds to the garden.*

Above: *A striking and unusual ornament like this will never be overlooked or ignored, but it needs careful placing in a small garden. Think carefully about the setting when choosing garden ornaments.*

Right: *You can create a sense of romance by using a classical figure among roses and other fragrant flowering plants. Be prepared to cut back the plants a little whenever they threaten to encroach over the figure and hide your focal point.*

Left: *Sometimes it is possible to combine an ornamental structure and interesting climbers at the same time. This arbour will look good from the moment you put it up, even before it's clothed with climbers. As shrubby climbers usually take a few years to look their best, plant some annual climbers at the same time for more immediate results. You could even plant runner beans, which have pretty flowers and an edible crop.*

Above: *This picture shows how a dull corner of the garden can be transformed by adding a figure or ornament: you don't necessarily need bold or brash colours to catch the eye. The focal point of the figure draws attention to the contrasting shapes and textures of the surrounding foliage.*

Sculpture

Garden sculpture plays a similar role to other garden ornaments, but it usually has a more artistic and individual interpretation. Choosing the pieces is all part of the pleasure, and something a little different will give your garden a touch of distinction.

Greek and Roman figures are still popular, but for the small modern garden, classical busts may look inappropriate. There are many alternatives that may be far more relevant to your garden style, and reflect your personality more closely.

Left: *A rusty wheel and a mannequin's hand may not immediately fire your imagination, but when reflected in a mirror set against the garden wall it can't fail to attract attention. A small diamond-shaped mirror has been hung between the two so that it glints as it turns.*

Below: *Some sculptures arrest the eye from across the garden, but this water and metal sculpture is one that you have to appreciate with close study. A feature like this will also serve as a watering place for birds, encouraging them to visit.*

Above: *Some sculptures look best set among plants, emerging from them with an air of mystery. This male torso has been turned modestly towards the wall.*

FAUX STONEWORK

If you can't afford expensive sculpture, use this ingenious paint effect to create a feature that looks old and interesting.

1 Sand the plastic mould to ensure the paint bonds well (use medium-grade paper), then paint all over with white acrylic primer. Let it dry for an hour or two, then paint over it with a coat of stone-coloured emulsion. Allow this to dry for two hours.

2 Tint some acrylic scumble glaze with a little raw umber, and thin with a little water before sponging it on to the mask. Leave for an hour or two until completely dry.

3 Tint some white acrylic paint with a small amount of yellow ochre. Add some scumble glaze then sponge on. Let it dry for an hour or two.

4 Tint some more white acrylic paint with burnt umber and thin with a small amount of water. Load an artist's brush and spatter it over the mask with a flicking movement. When it's dry, go over the whole thing with a matt Teflon-based polyurethane varnish.

Above: *This stone-effect wall mask, evocative of mediaeval times, amazingly started off as terracotta-coloured plastic.*

Lighting-up Time

One of the most dramatic instant improvements can transform your garden at the flick of a switch (or the lighting of a candle). Discover how magical your garden can be after dusk falls.

If you go out to work during the day, it's a pity to miss the pleasures of your garden, especially during the long winter months, when it may be dark when you leave and when you return. Even if you're able to enjoy the garden all day, you could be missing magical moments when dusk falls, and an illuminated garden takes on a whole new atmosphere and a sense of mystery which you may otherwise miss.

You don't have to flood your garden with the brilliance of security lighting; a much more subtle and atmospheric scene can be created by a softer, warmer glow. Individual features such as ornaments or spectacular plants can be picked out with small spotlights, with haunting shadows cast by leaves that dance with the breeze.

For summer evenings on the patio, candles and flares are essential and look fantastic.

Right: *Ornate lamps add a special elegance to the garden, and they can be used to provide practical illumination near a path as well as the more decorative contribution they make to the evening garden. A lamp like this will even be a feature during the day.*

Left: *Small lamps that cast their light downwards contribute a special atmosphere to the evening garden. This toadstool design is fun by day too.*

Above: *If you have a pond, make the most of the potential for interesting reflections – these flares are multiplied by the mirror effect of the water. It is also a good idea to have some form of illumination if you have deep water where people may walk after dark.*

THE PRACTICALITIES

Most permanent or semi-permanent garden lighting will need a power supply. Many low-voltage systems are available, and only a safe voltage is taken into the garden from a transformer indoors. But you still need to bury the cables in conduit to avoid the risk associated with trailing cables, especially in the dark.

Mains voltage lights are well worth considering if you plan to use your garden a lot in the evenings, but seek professional help to install them. Special weatherproof fittings have to be used and the armoured cable or cable in conduit has to be buried at a prescribed depth. This is not a do-it-yourself job unless you are particularly skilled and fully understand the relevant safety regulations.

Right: *A small lamp set among low-growing plants next to a path will double as a decorative feature during the day and a safety aid to mark the path after dark.*

Below: *Garden flares create a festive atmosphere, and are ideal for an evening party or supper on the patio. They provide a surprising amount of light, and some are scented to discourage insects.*

Bring in the Birds

Birds bring beauty, movement and melody to the garden, so try to encourage them. Nest boxes will help, and there's no reason why a nest box or bird house shouldn't be a feature in its own right: a home for the birds at nesting time, and a garden decoration all year round.

Apart from a palatial nest box, encourage birds into your garden with a supply of fresh water and wild bird food. They'll come to depend on this, so don't forget to put it out. Seedheads and berries will attract them, and they'll repay your hospitality by eating vast numbers of aphids and other garden pests.

MAKING A DAISY HOUSE

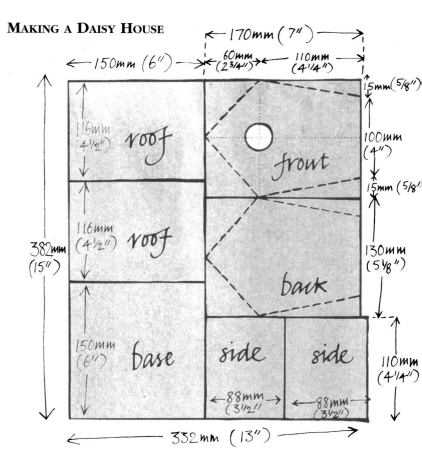

1 Using this cutting plan, mark out the basic house shape on 6 mm (¼ in) medium-density fibreboard (MDF) or exterior-grade plywood, and assemble with PVA glue and panel pins.

2 Using the template opposite as a guide, draw the flower, petal and leaf shapes on to the face of the board (or design your own). Measure and mark the position of the entrance hole.

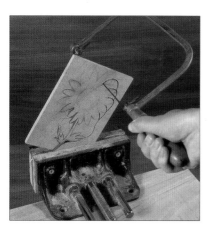

3 Cut out the shape with a coping saw. Remove the central hole in the motif using a padsaw after starting the hole with a drill. Paint the flower in appropriate colours, using emulsion paint. Use a fine brush to add detail.

4 Paint the house itself blue, then when dry apply the "grass" with a fine paintbrush. Paint the entrance hole yellow.

5 Use a glue gun to stick the flower and leaf shapes to the sides of the box. Paint the box with several coats of exterior-grade varnish. Make a support for the house and paint it green to match the grass around the sides.

Above: *If the woodwork decoration described for the daisy box sounds off-putting to you, simply build the basic box, then paint on a design. You can glue on a slice of cork to form a perch near the entrance.*

Left: *Use this template as a guide for a daisy design, or create your own if you fancy a different flower.*

Right: *An attractive bird house like this makes a delightful garden decoration as well as a welcome home for the birds.*

SHORT-CUT PLANTS

No matter how much you redesign your garden structurally, or how many decorations you add for instant impact, a garden needs plenty of plants. If your budget is big enough you can buy mature plants from specialist suppliers (exhibitors at garden shows use these to create instant "mature" gardens), but this is not normally a practical option, as the cost and labour involved is prohibitive. The impatient gardener needs other options for quick results.

FAST-GROWERS

Choose plenty of fast-growing plants, including trees and shrubs, that will put on a respectable show after a season or two and look reasonably robust in the meantime. Not all fast-growers are desirable, however, as many who have planted the Leyland cypress (x *Cupressocyparis leylandii*) have discovered.

Close planting can be very effective in making a group of plants look more mature than they really are. Provided the

Above: *Annuals are more than just cheap and cheerful flowers, they're essential for anyone looking for quick results while the slower plants become established. These pansies were coming into flower when bought, and have already been flowering for months, thanks to feeding and dead-heading.*

Left: *Hostas will take a few years to make a clump as large as this, but you can buy quite large specimens in garden centres that will put on a very respectable show in their first year.*

soil looks well covered, the fact that the plants have not reached their full height is not so important. You will need to buy more plants, and some may have to be removed or moved after a year or two, but your garden will look well clothed very quickly.

Using cheap, short-term gap-fillers, such as annuals, is another way to provide colour and interest while the slower growers are becoming established.

The plants suggested in the following pages won't try your patience while you're waiting for them to perform. Find the section that lists the type of plant you need, and use the suggestions as the basis of a short-list of plants to start with. These plants are mainly easy to grow, and unless otherwise stated they will tolerate a wide range of soils and grow in sun or partial shade.

Left: *Fennel may look like a feathery and fragile plant when you buy a seedling in spring, but by the end of the season it can be 1.8 m (6 ft) tall. The green and bronze forms in this picture were seedlings the previous year and are already about 60 cm (2 ft) high, only weeks after emerging in spring. Don't let it shed its seeds, otherwise you'll have a serious weeding job.*

Right: *Most spring-flowering bulbs will bloom in their first spring after planting, and many will continue to flower reliably in future years. These are* Anemone blanda, *which will form a carpet of early spring colour after a few years.*

Framework Trees and Shrubs

If you fill your garden with too many short-term plants, it will always lack a sense of maturity. Use some larger shrubs and small trees to provide height and a framework against which to view your other plants. The trees and shrubs suggested here can be bought at a mature stage to look attractive soon after planting, but they won't become too large for a small garden.

TREES TO TRY

Left: Pyrus salicifolia '*Pendula*'
The weeping willow-leaved pear remains small, and looks attractive and graceful even when young. It has small white flowers in spring and inconspicuous fruits later. It makes a nice specimen lawn tree.

Below: *Robinia pseudoacacia* 'Frisia'
The golden acacia is an outstanding small- to medium-sized tree suitable for most gardens. It retains its fresh golden colour throughout the summer, and looks very attractive even while still young and shrub-like.

Above: *Laburnum*
There are several species and hybrids of this popular small tree, but L. x watereri 'Vossii' (illustrated) is one of the very best.

USEFUL SHRUBS

Right: *Kerria japonica*
'Pleniflora'
Although not a choice shrub, this one is worth considering if you need a quick screen or a shrub to provide height. The shoots reach about 1.8 m (6 ft) or more, even when young. It tolerates most soils, and soon spreads into a large clump. The double yellow flowers appear in spring.

Below: *Amelanchier*
There are several forms of snowy mespilus that you might find in garden centres, all very similar and equally good: A. canadensis, A. laevis *and* A. lamarckii. *They have masses of small white flowers in spring and eye-catching autumn foliage colour. You will sometimes find them grown as a tree on a single stem, but usually they are grown as medium to large shrubs.*

Above: *Cornus alba*
There are many excellent varieties of this dogwood, invaluable for their year-round multiple merits. Some, like 'Elegantissima' (illustrated), are variegated, all have pleasing autumn leaf colour, and in winter the young red stems are a feature.

Quick Filler Shrubs

Whether you're planting a whole border with instant results in mind, or looking further ahead but need some fast-growers to make the border look clothed and interesting while the slower ones are becoming established, you won't be disappointed by the shrubs suggested here.

Filler shrubs, useful for making a newly planted border look clothed, and ideal for filling in a gap in an existing shrub border, have two essential qualities: fast growth and a bushy or upright shape. The ideal filler shrub also has attractive foliage that looks good while you're waiting for the flowers.

Below: *Lupinus arboreus*
The tree lupin does best on a light, sandy soil, but it's worth trying, provided your soil is not a heavy clay. The yellow flowers come in early summer, on stems that reach about 1.5 m (5 ft). Unlike the herbaceous border lupin, this is an evergreen branched shrub, albeit a short-lived one.

Left: *Lavatera*, shrubby type
You will find the shrubby or tree mallows under a variety of names, such as L. olbia, L. thuringiaca, or simply under a hybrid name such as 'Kew Rose' (illustrated). All are similar, with large pink flowers on tall stems that flower from early summer into autumn. This long-flowering shrub can reach 2.4 m (8 ft) or more, and the previous year's shoots should be cut back to within 15 cm (6 in) of the ground in early spring.

Above: *Fuchsia magellanica*
This hardy species has small flowers, and the top growth is likely to be killed in winter except in mild areas, but it readily shoots from the base in spring and makes a long-flowering and reliable bushy shrub. It usually grows to about 1.2 m (4 ft), taller in mild areas, and can simply be cut back to the ground in early spring. This is 'Aurea'.

Right: *Potentilla fruticosa*
There are many varieties and hybrids, mainly in shades of yellow, though some are pink or white. These unassuming plants remain compact at about 1.2 m (4 ft), but flower for a long period from early summer to early autumn, though midsummer is the peak flowering season. The variety illustrated is 'Goldstar'

Below: *Ligustrum ovalifolium* 'Aureum'
Better known as golden privet, this is often dismissed as a boring hedging plant. But it makes a super foliage shrub for a border, and can be clipped to keep it to a compact bush of about 1.5 m (5 ft).

In cold areas it may shed its leaves, but usually retains most of its bright foliage through the winter.

Above: *Philadelphus*
There are many beautiful philadelphus, all with white, fragrant flowers, but they vary considerably in height. Decide on the size you require, then ask your garden centre to recommend a suitable variety. The one illustrated is 'Virginal', which is a double variety that will grow to more than 1.8 m (6 ft).

Quick Focal Point Plants

Plants make excellent focal points when they are bold – and usually big. Shape and form can be as important as colour, but they must arrest the eye, even from across the garden, and stand out from their surroundings. It's worth considering all kinds of plants, from the giant brash annual sunflowers, to big ornamental grasses and the rocketing spires of some of the lovely ligularias.

BIG AND BOLD

Many trees make pleasing focal points, but they usually take years to reach a sufficient size to have much impact. Two palm-type plants that seldom fail to attract attention are the Chusan palm (*Trachycarpus fortunei*) and the cabbage tree (*Cordyline australis*), both of which are frost-hardy, provided the plants are reasonably mature and the winter not too severe. However, they will take years to look really impressive.

Many shrubs are eye-catching only while they're in flower, so consider those with attractive foliage too for a longer season of enjoyment.

Because the instant gardener is looking for speedy growth, many of the plants suggested here are annuals or biennials (the latter are sown one year to flower the next), or fast-growing perennials. For the perennials, don't expect an impressive display until at least their second season.

Left: *Alcea rosea*
The hollyhock is a traditional cottage-garden plant, not so often seen nowadays. Use it as a focal point at the back of a border, against the wall of a cottage, or anywhere that a "period" plant is required.
     Some modern varieties can be sown early in a greenhouse to flower in the first year, but the tall traditional kinds make better focal points. These are sown in spring or summer one year to flower the next. There are double varieties, but the singles are usually more striking from a distance. Flowering time is late summer and early autumn. Tall varieties grow to 2.4 m (8 ft).

Left: *Digitalis purpurea*
Foxgloves are among the select group of garden plants recognized by almost everyone, including non-gardeners. They flower in late spring and early summer, on spikes often 1.5–1.8 m (5–6 ft) tall, though some of the hybrids are more compact.

Right: *Gunnera chiliensis*
This architectural plant easily grows to 1.8 m (6 ft) and will be impressive even in its first year. It's most at home beside a pond, but will grow in a damp border if the soil is rich. For a small garden, choose G. tinctoria (*illustrated*). Winter protection for the crown is necessary in most areas.

Left: *Kniphofia*
There are many species of red-hot pokers, most of them with large and impressively spiky flowers on tall stems. Most are a mixture of red and yellow or orange and yellow, but some are mainly yellow. Choose a tall variety to make an eye-catching summer display.

Right: *Miscanthus sinensis* 'Zebrinus'
This large, clump-forming grass can be planted as a focal point at the back of a herbaceous or mixed border, or used as a specimen plant in a lawn. The leaves, which grow up to 1.2 m (4 ft), are transversely banded.

Above: *Cortaderia selloana*
Pampas grass needs little introduction, its tall silvery flower plumes being a familiar sight in autumn. The species itself may be too large for a small garden, as it makes a wide clump about 2.4 m (8 ft) high.

Above: *Helianthus annuus*
The common sunflower, so loved by children and still admired by most of us for its sheer size, shouldn't be overlooked where you need a quick-growing focal point for a season. There are now dwarf varieties too, so be sure to choose a tall one – these will normally grow to 2.4 m (8 ft) without any coaxing, taller with a little help.

Quick Ground Cover

Ground cover is usually planted to suppress weeds and keep maintenance to a minimum, but it should also be considered as a design feature in its own right. Blocks of ground cover plants provide a surface "texture" that can be used effectively to contrast with the mass of more solid and upright structures and plantings.

Most ground cover plants take a year or even two before they clothe the ground completely with a living carpet. But if you're impatient you can cheat and plant them closer together. Spread a mulch to suppress weeds until the plants grow.

Above: *Cerastium tomentosum*
Snow-in-summer is more usually associated with the rock garden or planted in a wall or bank, but it is useful for quick ground cover. The silvery-grey leaves are evergreen, but may not look very attractive in winter. It flowers in late spring and early summer.

Below: *Geranium endressii*
Although this cranesbill dies down in winter, it will provide dense summer cover. It's a desirable border plant in its own right, covered with pink flowers from early to late summer. 'Wargrave Pink' (illustrated) is a particularly good variety. Plant it in bold drifts.

Above: *Stachys byzantina*
The main attraction of lamb's tongue or lamb's ears is its grey, evergreen foliage, but it also has purple flowers in summer. The foliage produces a carpet about 15 cm (6 in) high.

Left: *Aubrieta deltoidea*
This popular rock plant is not often grown as ground cover, but it's useful where you want something quick and colourful. Unfortunately the plants become straggly after flowering, so you'll need to clip them over to remove seed heads and encourage compact growth. The usual height is about 15 cm (6 in). Plant in a sunny position on well-drained soil.

Above: *Hypericum calycinum*
The rose of Sharon is a tough ground cover that's a good choice for difficult positions such as banks. It will spread rapidly, so it's best used in an area where it can be confined, perhaps by a concrete path or the edge of a lawn. The plant grows to about 30 cm (12 in), and is covered with bright yellow flowers in mid and late summer. The foliage is almost evergreen, except in a severe winter.

Left: *Lamium maculatum*
This common plant is often overlooked because it's almost a weed in some gardens through self-sown seedlings and quick growth. But consider it for a wilder part of the garden where you need quick cover and you don't have to worry about it swamping choicer plants. Some varieties have white flowers, others silvery or even golden leaves.

Quick Climbers

The quickest climbers are likely to be annuals, but these are transient, and you'll probably want some permanent plants too. The best way to achieve cover in a hurry is to use a combination of annuals for rapid results, and perennials that will take over the following year.

If climbers are to be planted close to a wall or fence, take care to prepare the ground well and incorporate plenty of humus-forming and moisture-holding material, such as garden compost or rotted manure. Make the planting hole about 30 cm (1 ft) away from the support as it will almost inevitably cast a rain-shadow, causing dry soil. The stems can easily be angled and then trained towards the support.

Good ground preparation, careful planting, and regular watering are the keys to success if you want your climber to grow quickly.

Left: *Lathyrus odoratus*
The annual sweet pea needs no introduction. It's often grown for its fragrance and excellence as a cut flower, but it will make a pretty flowering temporary screen. Where height is needed in a border, sweet peas grown up netting secured to canes can become a focal point for several months.

ANNUAL CLIMBERS

Left: *Ipomoea*
There are several forms of morning glory, usually with large blue flowers. They have to be started in warmth indoors and carefully acclimatized before being planted out when there's no risk of frost, but growth can be rapid in a sheltered position.

Right: *Tropaeolum peregrinum*
The canary creeper is sometimes found under its synonym T. canariensis. Although it has masses of pretty yellow flowers, this is a leafy annual that's a good choice where you want to screen something. It's a more refined-looking plant than the related common nasturtium.

PERENNIAL CLIMBERS

Above: *Lonicera periclymenum*
For fragrance, the honeysuckle is difficult to beat among the perennial climbers, and it's one of those popular plants that everyone knows and loves. Plant early and late varieties to spread the flowering.

Below: *Vitis vinifera* 'Purpurea'
Grape vines can produce rapid and rampant growth, and you may want to consider a fruiting grape vine. It will grow very quickly in its second season. For an ornamental display, however, choose this variety, which is grown for its colourful leaves. It will reach over 6 m (20 ft).

Above: *Humulus lupulus* 'Aureus'
Few foliage climbers are as bright as the golden hop, with its curtain of golden leaves. The plant dies back for the winter, but regrows in spring and can reach more than 3 m (10 ft) in a season. Don't expect too much in the first year, but it will romp away afterwards.

Speedy Border Perennials

Herbaceous border plants sometimes take a season to become established, then they simply get bigger and better in succeeding years. But some will flower in their first year, and foliage plants start earning admiration from the moment their leaves emerge. Plant up your herbaceous border with an overall plan in mind, including plants you really like but that won't look spectacular for a year or two. Work in some of the plants suggested here to make your border look attractive right from the start.

Above: *Geranium* 'Johnson's Blue'
There are many blue-flowered species and hybrids that make stunning border plants and 'Johnson's Blue' is one of the best. The deep lavender-blue flowers are borne throughout the summer, and even young plants flower well. The normal height is about 30 cm (1 ft), sometimes a little taller.

Above: *Heuchera micrantha* 'Palace Purple'
A useful evergreen with a long summer flowering season, this purple-leaved plant is useful at the front of a border, and looks especially good in a drift in front of yellow-leaved plants. It does best in partial shade and on moisture-retentive but well-drained soil.

Right: *Aster novi-belgii*
Pretty Michaelmas daisies are invaluable for late colour in the border, the dwarf varieties such as 'Jenny' (illustrated) being typical of the modern dwarf varieties. They come mainly in blues, violets and pinks, and happily flower in autumn when most other border flowers have finished.

Right: *Papaver orientale*
Oriental poppies are show-offs that dominate the border when they're in flower in early summer. The big blooms come in many shades of red and pink, with some white varieties, on stems that grow to 60–90 cm (2–3 ft) depending on variety. Don't expect much of a show in their first year, but they'll probably look spectacular in their second season.

Below: *Lobelia cardinalis*
Although often used to add height for formal bedding schemes, this striking perennial lobelia makes a fine border plant. It will flower in its first season, and the dark, usually reddish-bronze, leaves make a feature in their own right. The spikes of deep red flowers in mid or late summer reach about 90 cm (3 ft).

Right: *Lupinus*
Lupins flower young, and you'll certainly have some spectacular flowers in early summer in the second season. The plants that are grown in borders are almost always hybrids, and you can buy named varieties (such as 'The Governor', illustrated) if you want to be sure of a particular colour. They do especially well on well-drained alkaline (chalky) soil, and prefer a sunny situation. Most grow to about 45–75 cm (1½–2½ ft).

Instant Summer Containers

Summer bedding plants are the impatient gardener's dream. They're often already flowering when you buy them, and within a couple of weeks they're bushy and blooming prolifically.

Those described here are easy and reliable plants that won't let you down. A few more unusual container plants are included along with old favourites, as every garden should have an element of surprise. Some of them are tender perennials and can be overwintered in a greenhouse if you wish, but they are usually bought as young plants in spring and discarded at the end of the season.

Left: *Nasturtium*
Botanically these are derived from Tropaeolum majus, but you'll almost always find them listed simply as nasturtium. Just sow where they are to flower.

Below: *Calendula*
Pot marigolds are one of the easiest hardy annuals to grow – simply sow the seed in spring where they're to flower, and they'll bloom in a month or two.

Left: *Diascia*
These have become popular plants in recent years, with greater availability and some fine hybrids. Their semi-trailing habit makes them a pleasing choice for baskets and windowboxes.

Although frost-hardy in the ground in many areas, plants in containers are best discarded at the end of the season (take cuttings to overwinter).

Left: *African marigold*
These bright showstopper plants used to be rather tall for containers, but they have been improved considerably in recent years, and now there are plenty of compact ones to choose from. The colours are mainly shades of yellow, though some have almost white flowers. You'll have more choice if you can raise your own plants from seed, but you can always buy plants from a garden centre. Although usually sold simply as African marigolds, some seed catalogues may list them under the Latin name Tagetes erecta. Tall varieties reach 75 cm (2½ ft), but dwarfs are as compact as 30 cm (1 ft).

Above: *Begonia semperflorens*
Fibrous-rooted begonias have all the qualities of a reliable container plant: they're compact, flower from early summer until the first frost, are not over-sensitive if they have to go without water for a day or two, and come in lots of bright colours often set off against glossy foliage.

Right: *French marigold*
One reason these bright plants are so popular is that they're usually in flower in the trays when you buy them at planting time, just begging to be bought. Another is their phenomenal flowering power: if deadheaded they will continue to bloom until the first frost.

Permanent Pot Plants

Seasonal plants, such as summer annuals and spring bulbs, will ensure your containers look beautiful for part of the year, but for a feeling of maturity around the year it's well worth planting some of your tubs with permanent plants. Just a few tubs or large pots planted with border perennials, shrubs, or even small trees, will give your garden a stronger sense of design and structure. These suggestions include a cross-section of the types of plants you should consider, even if some seem unlikely candidates.

Left: *Dahlia* (dwarf bedding type)
Many mail order catalogues and some garden centres offer tubers of dwarf dahlias suitable for containers (don't confuse these with the usually inferior seed-raised bedding dahlias). They will flower from mid or late summer until the first frost.

Store the tubers in a frost-free place, then replant the following season for a repeat performance.

Below: *Chrysanthemum* (dwarf patio type)
These naturally dwarf and bushy varieties are really easy to grow, and will be covered with flowers in all the usual chrysanthemum colours between early and late autumn, depending on variety.

Right: *Syringa vulgaris*
Lilac seems an unlikely choice for a tub, as those planted in the ground often grow tall and are frequently sparse at the base. But you can buy plants already coming into flower in spring, and these make unusual container shrubs.

Above: *Fatsia japonica*
One of these large evergreen shrubs with its bold outline will provide your patio or garden with interest at any time of the year, and this is one shrub well worth trying. Mature plants have unusual rounded heads of white flowers in late autumn. It's unlikely to grow to much more than about 1.8 ft (6 ft) in a tub.

Above: *Viburnum tinus*
Laurustinus is often dismissed as a boring shrub, but it has many merits. The evergreen foliage is unexciting during the summer, but the plant will bear white or pink flowers from early winter right through to early spring.
    Specimens planted in the ground can grow tall, but in a tub it will remain compact.

Left: *Rhododendron* hybrids
These popular shrubs require an acid soil, so if you garden in an alkaline (chalky) area, growing them in tubs may achieve the best results. Fill the container with an ericaceous compost (which will be acidic). Plants are often sold already in flower.

Above: Laburnum and *Acer platanoides*
Use small trees in large pots to provide your patio planting with a vertical element. This laburnum (right) should do well in a container, being a small tree. The Acer platanoides 'Drummondii' (left) will soon demand more space.

The Beauty of Bulbs

Bulbs, and the majority of corms and tubers, are sure-fire packaged plants that will burst into bloom within six months of planting, sometimes even sooner. Many kinds will make bigger and bolder clumps year by year.

Most gardeners plant spring-flowering bulbs, but you shouldn't ignore those that flower in summer and autumn. You can have these plants in flower every month of the year, and most of them are trouble-free and easy to grow. Often you can make the clumps look more established simply by planting the bulbs close together.

Right: Tulips
These are among the world's best-known flowers, but there are many kinds, from dwarf species to large and showy hybrids. Some flower as early as late winter or early spring, others in mid or late spring. Heights vary from about 15 cm (6 in) to over 60 cm (2 ft).

Below: *Narcissus*
This huge group of spring-flowering bulbs includes the large-flowered daffodils, growing to 45 cm (18 in) or more, and small species such as N. cyclamineus, along with many hybrids of the small-flowered species. Narcissi naturalize well and will usually grow into large clumps over the years if the bulbs are left undisturbed.

SPRING BULBS

Left: *Crocus*
Crocuses need no introduction, and the numbers planted each year testify to their popularity. Plant them in autumn and forget them until the spring. Crocus chrysanthus (illustrated) often flower in late winter.

Above: *Hyacinth*
Hyacinths can be in flower very quickly in the home, especially if you buy prepared (treated) bulbs, but ordinary hyacinths are invaluable for a spring display in the garden. Varieties vary in their earliness, so check before you buy.

SUMMER AND AUTUMN BULBS

Left: *Crocosmia*
These make super border plants, with mid to late summer flowers in shades of red, orange or yellow, eventually making a dense clump and growing to about 60–90 cm (2–3 ft). They will flower in their first season, but the best show will be in subsequent years.

Right: *Colchicum*
These so-called autumn crocuses are not true crocuses, but the large flowers have a typical crocus shape. There are several widely available species and hybrids (the one illustrated is C. nudiflorus), blooming mainly in early and mid autumn.

Above and left: Dahlia
There are dahlias compact enough for a windowbox, and giants over 1.5 m (5 ft) high with huge blooms almost the size of dinner plates. There are sure to be some that are right for your garden. Plant the tubers when frost is unlikely to damage emerging shoots. They will flower mainly in late summer and autumn, though some dwarfs will be in flower by midsummer.

Water Plants

Some popular pond plants, such as waterlilies, take several seasons before they look well established, but there are plenty of plants that will make your pond look well-planted and mature in a surprisingly short time. Some you need only float on the water and leave to multiply. Beware of fast growers such as duckweed, which will quickly become an annoying weed. Some of those mentioned below multiply rapidly, but they are very easy to control by cutting or raking out surplus growth.

Above: *Elodea canadensis*
Canadian pondweed couldn't be easier to grow or faster to multiply. You just place it in the water (preferably anchored with a weight to ensure it sinks), and leave it to grow and spread.

Right: *Houttuynia cordata*
One of the most adaptable pond and garden plants, it will grow in a dryish border, a boggy area, or planted slightly submerged on the marginal shelf of your pond. It will die down in winter, but produces plenty of foliage in summer. The variety illustrated is 'Flore Pleno'. 'Chameleon' is an especially good variety with multi-coloured leaves.

Left: *Pistia stratiotes*
It's easy to see why this is called the water lettuce. Buy the tender plants in early summer and float them on the surface of your pond – you'll soon have a worthwhile colony. They can be overwintered in warmth, but it's easier to start afresh each year.

Right: *Caltha palustris*
The marsh marigold or kingcup, with its bright yellow blooms in spring, is ideal for the marginal shelf of your pond (or the bank of a stream if you have one running through your garden). It will flower young and is easy to establish. There is also an attractive double form.

Above: *Mimulus*
The yellow monkey flower, M. luteus, grows vigorously beside streams or in shallow water, but the many hybrids are more decorative and colourful, often in shades of red or orange. Most of these will grow happily in damp soil or at a pond edge.

Right: *Aponogeton distachyos*
While you're waiting for a waterlily to become sufficiently established to flower properly, the water hawthorn will have been flowering prolifically, putting on a respectable performance in its first year, with scented white flowers from spring until well into autumn.

EASY GARDEN CARE

Quick-response gardening involves more than simply choosing plants that grow quickly or flower young. They need a certain amount of nurturing and encouraging to get off to a good start. Care and attention works surprisingly well in persuading normally reluctant plants to put on that vital vigorous spurt of growth while they're still young. A year on, one that's fed and watered regularly may end up twice the size of another that's received a severe check to growth through neglect.

Those chores that are easily put off, like weeding and mulching, will not only help your plants to grow faster and better, as there will be less competition from weeds, but your beds and borders will look smarter too.

WATERING

With water economy in mind, it's easy to find an excuse not to water new plants as often as you should, but there are better ways to save water.

An established lawn may turn brown in a drought, but it will almost certainly revive when the rains return. A well-established shrub or border plant may wilt and look unattractive, but it probably won't be killed. On the other hand, a young plant struggling to become established could easily become a dead one, or at best will be retarded and slow to grow afterwards. Concentrate your watering efforts on new plants, even if you have to neglect some of the older ones (which you can help by mulching, for example).

If you find watering a chore, install a self-watering system, or use one that's permanently in position and just needs turning on at the tap. There are many

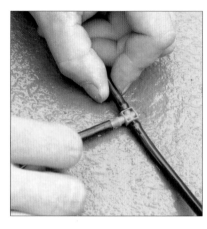

systems from which to choose, some based on sprinklers, others on drips from a nozzle, yet more from pipes through which the water slowly oozes. Sprinklers are probably the least effective for a border in terms of water wastage. Drip feeds are more economical with water than sprinklers.

Below: *Drip heads are positioned close to plants to be watered. The rate of delivery is usually easy to adjust to suit individual plants.*

Above: *Most automatic watering systems have a control system to reduce the water pressure, and some act as a filter to prevent nozzles becoming clogged.*

FEEDING

The easiest way to ensure new plants don't go short of nutrients is to incorporate a slow-release or controlled-release fertilizer into the planting area. These will ensure a constant supply of nutrients for several months.

Hoeing in a general garden fertilizer at planting time and again a couple of months later is another way to ensure good nutrition.

If you forgot to do this, or your plants are simply starting to look jaded, try applying a liquid fertilizer that can be absorbed by both foliage and roots, at the rate recommended by the manufacturer. These are usually fast-acting.

Left: *Drip-feed watering systems are very versatile, and junction pieces are available to enable the pipes to be run to wherever they are required.*

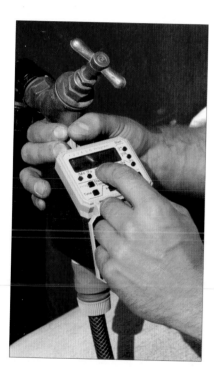

Above: *Some automatic watering systems are controlled by the moisture in the soil, others maintain a continuous drip while the water source is turned on. A timing device like the one shown is useful for those not operated by soil moisture. It can be turned off during wet weather.*

Below: *These two tomato plants demonstrate the effectiveness of good feeding. Both were planted in an identical potting mixture, and received the same day-to-day care, but the one on the left had an additional dose of slow-release fertilizer. After just a couple of months the benefit is obvious, and feeding will have a similar effect on most of what you plant.*

WEEDING

Digging and pulling out weeds by hand is very effective but not a job many of us enjoy. Hoeing is less tiring and perfectly satisfactory for annual weeds or the seedlings of perennials. It isn't so effective for difficult deep-rooted weeds.

Chemical control with herbicides can be useful, but it's important to choose one that's appropriate, and essential to be careful about spray drifting on to desirable plants. Some modern weedkillers are non-persistent in the soil, making it possible to replant very soon after application. Some are effective for annual weeds and seedlings, acting like a chemical hoe; others are carried though the plant's vascular system to all parts and will kill even persistent problem weeds, though more than one application may be necessary. Always read the pack details and instructions very carefully and be sure to use weedkillers only for the weeds and situations recommended by the manufacturer – if killing lawn weeds, for example, make sure you use one formulated specifically for lawns.

Right: Hoeing is a very effective method of weed control except for very difficult persistent weeds. A traditional long-handled hoe is usually used, but small tools like this onion hoe can be used in a confined area.

Above: If treating weeds with a herbicide, screen neighbouring plants to ensure none of it drifts on to desirable plants.

Above: Deep-rooted weeds are best treated with a translocated weedkiller such as one based on glyphosate. Use a gel formulation to paint on to the leaves if there's a risk of a spray affecting neighbouring plants.

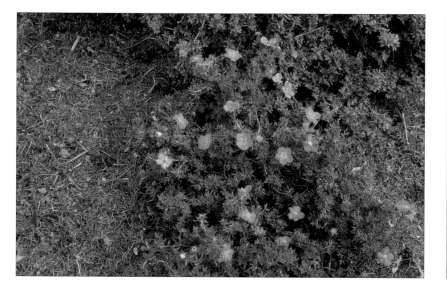

Above: *Grass clippings make a cheap and effective mulch, but don't apply them more thickly than about 5 cm (2 in), and don't use any from lawns treated with a weedkiller.*

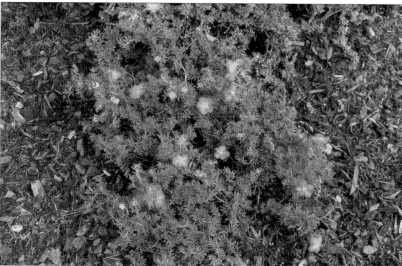

Above: *Chipped or composted bark is a popular choice because it's visually acceptable, widely available, and efficient as a mulch.*

MULCHING

There are many merits to mulching. Provided the ground is moist before you apply the material, it will help to conserve moisture and mean you have to water less often. It will suppress weeds, so reducing competition for light and water. And most kinds of mulch will visually improve the appearance of the bed after planting. Those that aren't attractive, such as plastic sheets, can be covered with a thin layer of something like chipped bark to improve their appearance. Loose mulches on their own should be at least 5 cm (2 in) thick.

Left: *Black plastic and mulching sheets are not the most attractive garden accessory, but can be improved visually with a layer of gravel or chipped bark.*

Above: *Black plastic or a special mulching sheet works very efficiently. It's usually laid first, then slits are made to plant through it.*

Index